Old Cat Care

Kurt Indermaur

Old Cat Care

Kurt Indermaur

ISBN 978-1-7330599-1-6

Leanpub

This is a Leanpub book. Leanpub empowers authors and publishers with the Lean Publishing process. Lean Publishing is the act of publishing an in-progress ebook using lightweight tools and many iterations to get reader feedback, pivot until you have the right book and build traction once you do.

To the old cats who patiently teach us, and to the kittens who benefit from the lessons we learn. May we always give them our best.

Contents

First Things First

What is an old cat?

It seems like a simple question, doesn't it?

But what is "old?" In particular, what is "old" for a cat? Is it a cat that is considered "senior" by the pet food industry, more than 7 years old? Is it more than that? 10 years? 15? 20?

No.

The answer is not your cat's age in years, but your cat's age as she[1] tells it to you.

Does she need you more?

When she is young, caring for her is easy. You set out food and water and clean the litter box, and she pretty much takes care of herself. She might curl up next to you on a cold day, or follow you in the garden, or nag you when she wants something, but for the most part she does fine on her own.

Then she reaches a point where she sleeps a little longer, or lingers in a warm spot when before she would have moved on. She is a little less adventurous, more interested in comfort than the thrill of a hunt. She purrs just as much, but she runs a little less, jumps not quite so high, with more effort. She might even lose a little weight. She is not yet old, but she is getting older.

You settle into a comfortable routine. A few years go by and it seems like nothing will change, but one year the days will get cooler and

---

[1]Throughout this book I refer to my old cat and your old cat as "she." I could not refer to any cat as "it," and I have had old cats of both sexes. I finally chose 'she' because my oldest cat, Teddy, was female, and it helped me to think of her as I wrote.

you will notice her gait stiffen in her hind legs. She will avoid higher places so she won't have to jump down. She will pause before going down stairs. Her eating and drinking habits may change. She might prefer to drink from a faucet instead of bending down to a bowl. She may no longer be able to groom herself as thoroughly as she used to.

Each cat is an individual, as unique in her health and longevity profile as she is in her personality. Some cats live long lives, while others die young. Some stay healthy almost to the ends of their lives while others suffer long, slow declines. But no matter how old your cat is, or even if she is not old yet, she will need your help someday, and when she does this book will help you do your best for her.

How do you know when she needs you?

Cats do not often ask for help. If you have a cat who is very expressive, very needy - consider yourself lucky! It is much easier to know when she needs you.

But more often, her stubborn independence can easily mislead you into thinking that nothing is wrong. She works hard to conceal her weakness, and may retreat from you if she is sick or in pain. You do not need to be a hypochondriac for her, but you do need to be attentive.

The best way to know when she needs you is to spend time with her. The more time you spend with her, the more you will know what is "normal" for her - from where she likes to spend her time: up high, on the bed, tunneled under a blanket, in the sun; to what she likes to eat and drink, how much, how often; and so on. You will get to know her weight, the condition of her coat and skin, her eyes, nose, mouth and ears. The more you know what is "normal" for her, the easier it will be to notice a change.

To be sure, when she does change, it is not always a sign of trouble. She may simply be telling you she *wants* a change. But the most important thing is to pay attention. By making a change, she is inviting you to deepen your relationship - to get to know her better

- to understand the reasons for her change. When she changes, start by asking yourself:

- What is changing? Is it her behavior, her physical condition, or both?
- Is the change gradual, or sudden?
- Is it a small change, or a big one?
- Is the change a matter of choice, or necessity?
- Is the change temporary, or does it appear to be permanent?

Start with empathy and curiosity, then work toward understanding. If you need help, by all means read and ask online, and do not hesitate to consult your veterinarian, too!

How to raise an old cat

Old cats are not born that way. They are raised from a very early age to live longer, and all those good habits you develop in caring for them make it easier - for both of you - in their old age.

The good news is that it is not complicated. You just have to be consistent: take good care of her every day. You also do not have to get it perfect. You just have to start, and try to get better. And if you fall back - if you find yourself doing less than you think you can - just pick yourself up and get a little better **today**.

I will go into more detail in the rest of the book, especially in how to change as your cat gets older, but if your cat is still young you can lay a solid foundation of health by following a few simple guidelines.

Food

Feed her the best food you can - as close to a natural, wild diet as you can. Cats are carnivores. Feed your cat raw food if you can, high quality protein - *meat*. Read labels and look for real meat first, not "by-products," not "meal," not corn or rice. Start where you can, and strive to get better. And if you are not sure what "better" is, watch your cat. If her coat gets softer, thicker and shines; if her eyes sparkle; if she is more energetic and playful, then her food is probably better.

Activity

I know cats like to sleep a lot more than people, but they still like to run and jump and hunt and chase, and they get bored and listless without it. Or they will pace. Or get irritable. Or pester you when *you* want to sleep.

If you can give your cat access to a safe outdoor environment, do it. Seeing birds and bugs and blowing leaves - and wind and rain and snow and sun - gives her an endless stream of ever-changing rooms to play in. If you can have more than one cat, they can play with each other, or at least talk.

When you are with her, you can play. It does not have to be anything fancy, just a string, a cardboard tube, crumpled paper, a ping pong ball - be creative, and keep her moving.

Care

When she is done playing, pet her, brush her, comfort her, talk to her. Let her know you care. More than that, keep her safe - outside or inside, away from cars and wild animals outside, from choking hazards and cleaning solutions inside.

She should not be a stranger to the vet, either, and neither should you. Ideally, you should be able to talk to your vet about your cat's diet, behavior, exercise and litter box habits, what you have read on the internet, what foods you are trying. And your vet should talk to you as an equal partner in caring for your cat - you are there for her every day, and your vet has the training, expertise and experience to spot trouble, assess information and guide you and your cat to a long-term, mutually healthy life.

Your care for your cat should be an everyday habit - which should be easy and enjoyable. But I know that life has a way of interrupting, of sidelining good intentions. Or you may have multiple cats (I hope you do), and some may be more sociable - may come find you - and others more retiring. Whatever their personalities cats are not meant to be entirely alone.

If you have more than one cat, it is probably worth reflecting on a regular basis - weekly - on how much time you spend with each of your cats. If you feel it is not enough, the next week turn more toward the cat you have been neglecting - grooming and petting her, playing with her and lying beside her. I find repeated, gentle redirecting works much better for me than setting a hard goal and feeling guilty or beating myself up about missing it.

If you work all day, and no one else is home with your cat, then it is even more important to turn toward your cat (work, email, phone and TV can all wait). It will be better *for you*, too, to spend some quiet time purring with your cat.

Why care for an old cat?

A more direct way of asking the question might be, "How much would you do for your cat?" or "How much is too much?" or "When have you done enough?" But these are very personal, emotionally charged questions, and the answers can only be speculative - who knows what they might do when faced with a life-or-death decision?

So I ask you to take a step back and not just consider *what* you would be willing to do for your cat, but *why* you would be willing to do it. Why do you *want* to take care of your cat in her old age?

If you are reading this book, you may have already answered this question for yourself. But if you have not, it is worth a little self-examination to try to understand your reasons before you are in the middle of whatever burdens - physical, emotional or financial - that caring for your old cat might bring. If you think about it now, and discuss it with your loved ones, you may be better prepared to decide what to do when caring for your old cat becomes more difficult.

Here are some avenues to explore.

Are you caring for your old cat...

Because you love her?
- Because you care for her?
- Because she needs you?
- Because you can - you have the time and resources to do it?

Because you owe it to her?
- Because she has given you years of love and companionship?
- Because you want to make up for past mistakes you have made?
- Because you have promised a friend?

Because you want to learn from her?
- Because you want to learn how to care for others?
- Because you want to learn how to show compassion?
- Because you want to learn how to ease suffering?
- Because you want to learn how to die?

Because you love life?
- Because life is precious and short?
- Because you want more kindness in the world, and less suffering?
- Because you want more compassion in the world, and less hard-heartedness?

*Because **she** loves life?*

- Because she has a strong will to live?
- Because she has always had joy in living?

If you are anything like me, you will not have a single answer, but a mix, some more important, some less that will evolve over time.

In my experience, cats - especially old cats - are incredibly patient and tolerant of our care of them, no matter how clumsy or inept we may be. If we are willing to learn, they are great teachers. As you care for your old cat, you will develop your own gentleness, patience and attentiveness, and learn to:

- Read signs of sickness and health, even when your patient cannot speak.
- Accept with grace the inevitability of suffering, illness and death.
- Appreciate the essential beauty of life itself, even when external appearances fade.

By her example, your cat will show you how to live through difficulties, how to handle dying, how to tolerate your clumsiness with forbearance - how to love you through her pain. And you, in your turn, will be given an opportunity to show your love for her - not the easy love of happy times, but the deep, self-sacrificing love that lays you bare, that forces you to face your limitations - to face your limitations and keep going in spite of them, for her. In the end, if you are lucky, you will also learn a little more about yourself.

Can I do it?

Caring for an old cat is not for everyone. It is not always easy. It can take a lot of time. It can be emotionally draining. It can be...

messy. There are times you may want to travel, but she needs you. You may be out for an evening, but you cannot stay out long - you need to get back to her.

But if you can make those choices, after a while you will not even think about it. Your priorities will shift. You will want to be with her first, and you will not even consider anything else. In return, you will get... heartache, but also genuine tenderness, a deep appreciation for life in all its strength, and all its fragility, and first-hand experience of the nobility inside every individual (in your cat, that is, and maybe even in you).

Others may question your judgment: "Why are you doing this?" "Wouldn't it be easier to just have her 'put to sleep'?" Of course death can be difficult to face, especially if it does not come quickly, but that is no reason to deny it - or rush it. Be prepared for some to criticize your choice to care for an older cat, but remember that you are not alone. Seek out others, including veterinarians, who support your decision to help your cat, not by ending her life, but by sustaining it as much as possible.

There is no need to feel defensive about your choice, no need to explain. Do not try to convince anyone who disagrees. Just know yourself, and be willing to go deeper than you expect in caring for your cat, and you will learn more about her - and yourself - than you imagined.

Once you have made that choice, be honest with yourself. Ask yourself the following questions, and double-check your answers with someone who knows you well. Caring for an old cat is not easy for anyone, but if you have trouble answering "yes" to more than a few of these, it may be more than you can handle. If that is the case and you still want to try, at least consider where you might need help, and be prepared to ask for help sooner rather than later.

Can you give medical care?

You may need to give minor medical care - bathing, pills, shots. If you have never done what is required before, your vet can coach you. A mobile vet may also be available who can coach you in your own home. Once you know how to do what needs to be done, you will be able to provide better care - immediately (no waiting for an appointment) and at home (no office visit required), which is much easier on your cat - and on you.

Can you be gentle?

You will need to be firm, but gentle in providing medical care. But you will also need to be gentle if you need to help your cat eat, or groom, or to massage her arthritic joints without hurting her.

Can you get dirty?

You will also need to be comfortable getting close to your cat - without squeamishness. Medical conditions may make her look or smell unpleasant. Can you collect stool samples? Can you clean up after diarrhea, or vomiting?

Are you patient?

Sometimes your old cat may have trouble eating, or may have lost her appetite. You may need to help her eat, or revive her appetite. This could mean that her usual five-minute feeding time stretches to ten minutes or more. Can you do that without getting frustrated? She may pee and poop outside of her box repeatedly. Can you clean that up without getting irritated (or at least controlling your irritation)?

Do you have time?

You may need to help her eat several times a day, or help her move from one place to another, or get her a heating pad to make her more comfortable. Do you have time to attend to her?

Do you have endurance?

If she needs you, will you be able to get up in the middle of the night one time, three times, five times - for months at a time?

Are you persistent?

If she is uncomfortable, or not eating, or keeps going outside her box, will you keep working to find a solution that works for her - and you?

Are you attentive to detail?

If you do not know what is normal, you cannot tell if anything is getting worse - or better. The slightest change in her condition may need your - or your vet's - care. Will you notice?

Are you empathetic?

Can you learn to read the signs in her body almost as if it were your own? Can you figure out what is bothering her when she cannot tell you?

Are you responsible?

She is counting on you. She may have no one else. Can she trust you to take care of her, even when it is difficult?

Are you humble?

You will do your best, but do you know when to ask for help? Learn from everyone you can - your vet, your vet's assistants, other cat owners, dog owners, books, online. **Learn from your old cat.**

And finally...

Can you do all of the above with hope, kindness and love, still knowing that she will die? You may not be able to relieve her discomfort entirely. You will not be able to cure her. Your best will not be enough to save her. At some point all you will be able to do is be there for her. Can you do that for her?

I won't sugar-coat it. Even if you can do all that - be all that - for your cat, it will not be easy. It will not always be pleasant, and it will end in death. But there will be rewards - for your cat and for you.

Facing death each day helps you decide what is really important to you, and refine it day by day. Opening your heart to pain, and working through it, makes your heart bigger, stronger and more charitable. All the patience and kindness and empathy you practice in caring for your cat spills over into the rest of your life.

And you will discover that memories - deep, lasting, happy memories - can still be found in all the little ways she appreciates all the little things you do for her.

How to care for your old cat

So you have made it this far - you have raised an old cat. Congratulations! Your cat thanks you.

But now she needs you more. She may be just as forgiving as ever of your mistakes, but her body is not. Over the years of your lives together, you have learned what to expect from her: how much she eats and drinks, what her normal poops and pees look like, and so on. To keep her at her best you will not only have to continue the great care that has gotten you this far. But you will also have to be even more attentive to her needs, and even more aware of any changes to her health.

To help you, in this section I offer practical suggestions for your old cat's care, grouped by category. For each category I cover:

- *Basics* - to keep your cat at her best
- *What to watch* - to spot signs of potential problems
- *Hints & techniques* - to help you overcome common challenges

Food

Your cat needs food that tastes good, that is good for her, and is easy to digest. For my cat, that has ended up being grain-free canned food that is a fine pâté, easily diluted with water - to make it even easier to eat, and to keep my cat well hydrated. For a treat, I give her chopped up chicken breast, or sometimes a little canned tuna or salmon with plenty of juice.

But it is important that you find your own cat's favorite foods and respond to her tastes. She may like chicken-based food for a while, then switch to seafood, or rabbit or duck or lamb.

Keep an eye on her weight, as well as on the size and consistency of her stools, and adjust her food accordingly.

You can give her supplements, but I don't like to rely on them. Better to give her a strong base diet, and use supplements only as... supplements. And be careful – most supplements will change the taste or smell of food, and your cat may not appreciate the change. Once an older cat stops eating, it can be nerve-wracking until you get her to start eating again.

Basics

A more natural diet
Start reading ingredient labels on the food she eats. Look for meat first, not "meal," not "by-products," but "chicken" (or whatever her meat of choice is). If you see lots of non-meat ingredients near the beginning of the list, find another food. If you see ingredients you don't recognize, learn about them. If you see ingredients that seem like they might have something to hide, like "by-products," try to find food without them.

Variety
Some people swear by a particular brand, and others warn you to

be careful about changing your cat's diet, but I find that no matter what brand or flavor or meat they love, they will get bored with it. There is also a risk, admittedly small, that if you stick with a single brand or protein source, your cat might either (a) get too little of an important nutrient[2] or (b) get too much of an ingredient that could harm their health.[3] The effects of both deficiencies and harmful ingredients tend to accumulate gradually over time. If you feed her a variety of high-quality foods, she is more likely to stay interested in eating, and avoid any detrimental effects she she may experience with one particular food.

Texture

As your cat gets older, you may find that she has more trouble swallowing chunks or flaked or shredded food. Pâté is easier for her to lap up, and if you ever need to feed her with a syringe (see *Hints* below), a finely-ground pâté works best.

Supplements

I have had some success with glucosamine/chondroitin supplements to help with joint stiffness, but for the others I have tried - vitamins, probiotics, enzymes - I have not noticed enough of a difference to make them worth the cost, or the risk that she stops eating because of the funny taste of the supplement. Supplements often change the taste of the food enough that she stops eating until I stop the supplement.

What to Watch

Is she eating more or less than usual?

Your cat's appetite can be an easy-to-read sign of how she is feeling. If she will not eat, and nothing is wrong or different with her food, something is bothering her. If her behavior changes but she still eats as usual, you should still figure out what is causing it, but her healthy appetite will support her while you figure it out.

---

[2]Like taurine deficiency in cat foods in the 1970s
[3]Like the 2007 melamine pet food poisoning scandal

Has she lost or gained weight?
Remember that your cat - even if she is a very large cat - is not very big. Even a pound or two can make a big difference in the health of your cat. If she is gaining weight, then slowly, gradually feed her less. If she is losing weight, try encouraging her to eat more, or find a food she likes more. If she continues to lose weight, **see your vet**.

Is she throwing up? More than usual?
Vomiting could be a serious health problem - maybe even caused by the food. Or it could be as simple as a hairball, or grass. You will have to judge, based on your cat's history, if vomiting is unusual for her. If you have any doubt, talk to your vet.

Hints & techniques

Mix in extra water
Older cats often drink less water than they need. Adding water to her food makes the food easier to eat **and** makes her water taste better, too.

Warm it slightly
Your older cat's sense of smell may not be as good as it once was, and her food, especially if it has been refrigerated, may not have much smell, either. Adding warm water, or warming it for a few seconds in the microwave (touch it with a finger to make sure it is not too hot) can kick up the smell enough to pique her interest. Or if her food will be eaten within a day, you can keep it covered on the counter (at room temperature) to make it more appetizing.

Touch food to her lips
Touching food to her lips will trigger her to lick her lips and taste her food, and that may whet her appetite enough that she will continue to eat more on her own.

Tuna juice
She will not get complete nutrition from tuna juice, but it has a combination of strong odor and taste that many cats find irresistible.

You can use tuna juice alone, or put tuna juice over her regular food. Try it both ways and find out which one your cat prefers.

Grated parmesan cheese
Before you try grated parmesan cheese, make sure she does not have irritable bowel syndrome or any other sensitivity to dairy products. Like tuna juice, parmesan has a strong odor and taste that can easily be sprinkled over food to get your cat started eating again.

Raise her food bowl
If your cat has arthritis or any other condition that limits her flexibility, she many benefit from having her food bowl raised. You can start out holding it for her to find what height works best, and then figure out a structure to hold it for you. For some cats, lowering their head to eat can lead to vomiting. Raising their food bowls can make that less likely.

A wider, shallower food bowl
Your cat may prefer to eat out of a wider bowl that does not brush against her whiskers, or a shallower bowl that does not require her to push her face into her food. As a side benefit, her face will stay cleaner, too.

Tilt her food bowl
Your cat may also find it easier to eat if you tilt her bowl slightly toward her. If you have mixed her food with water, the liquid will be easier to lap up, pooled to one side of her bowl.

Use a syringe
If all else fails, you can use a large syringe to draw up a slurry of food and gently squirt it into your cat's mouth. A hard plastic syringe will work, but flexible, silicone-tipped syringes are much easier to work with, and your cat will not mind nearly as much.

It is difficult and time-consuming to feed a cat this way, but sometimes it is the only way that works. When it goes well, after a time it can revive her interest in food and she will start eating again on her own.

Try an appetite stimulant

Ask your vet if there is a medication you could try to stimulate your cat's appetite. Your vet will be able to check for underlying conditions, and balance treatments for your cat's underlying conditions with treatments for her lack of appetite.

Water

Your cat should always have easy access to clean, fresh water. As she gets older, she may be less willing to move as far for water, or declining kidney function may lead to more urination - and therefore a greater need for water to avoid dehydration. Or she may seek out warmer spots in the sun, on a heating pad or in front of the fire, which can also dry her out. Dehydration can be insidious, creeping up on your cat a little at a time, and it can take a while to get things back in balance, so it pays to be vigilant.

Basics

Clean water
A simple bowl of water changed at least daily (I like to change it once in the morning and once at night) gives your cat a good foundation. Do not forget to check that her bowl is clean, too - and wash it frequently.

Accessible
Put her water where she can get to it easily, where she feels safe when she drinks, and where it will not get contaminated too easily - far enough from food and litter boxes, for example.

What to Watch

Is she well hydrated?
Extreme dehydration is easy to spot - sunken eyes, dull coat, listless behavior, but you want to notice it well before it is an emergency. Luckily, there is a simple "pinch test" you can use any time to gauge your cat's hydration.

Just take a small fold of skin between two fingers and release it - I like to do it just behind her shoulders. If it snaps back quickly, no problem. If it takes longer - a second or two - she needs more water. Longer than that, she should see a vet.

Like all of your other monitoring, you should "pinch test" on a regular basis. That way you'll get a good baseline, to understand what is "normal" for your cat when she is healthy, and you can be sure when it takes longer that something is amiss.

Is she drinking more or less?
Paradoxically, drinking a lot of water can also be a sign of health problems in your cat, but not necessarily. The key to watch for is: Has her drinking **changed** from her usual frequency and amount? To know that you have to know what's usual for her.

If you have one cat it is easier - you can simply check the water level in her bowl when you refill it. But if you have multiple pets you will need to take note of when she drinks and for how long.

Is she peeing more or less?
You can get a pretty good idea of the volume of your cat's urine from what she leaves in the litter box. But sometimes it is also useful to get a look at the color of her urine (see *Collecting urine samples* under *Hints & Techniques*, below). Urine that is dark, or too yellow, or not yellow enough might be signs of health issues worth discussing with your vet.

Hints & Techniques

Raise her water bowl
If your older cat suffers from arthritis, she might have trouble getting down low enough to drink from her bowl. Raising her bowl just a few inches will make it easier and more accessible for her.

Use a water fountain
Some cats prefer moving water. If your cat has enjoyed drinking from a sink or bathtub faucet, she may like drinking from a fountain. A small recirculating pump is all you need. The moving

water can also be filtered to keep cat hair or bits of food out of her water.

Add flavor to her water

Your cat may drink more water if it has some odor, some flavor. A small bit of liquid from a can of tuna or chicken, or even her favorite food, can make her bowl of water more appealing. As a side benefit, the flavor can also whet her appetite for more food if she has been losing weight.

Burp your cat (like a baby)

If it is a struggle for her to bend down, or difficult for her to swallow, your cat may swallow air along with her water. You may notice this if she fidgets, if she can't seem to get comfortable after eating and drinking. She may burp on her own, or may throw up a little. You can help her burp up the air by simply petting her back until she purrs, with an occasional light finger tap.

Use a (large) syringe

If your cat is not drinking enough water on her own, you can get a large (10cc) syringe and gently squirt water into her mouth 1 or 2 cc's at a time. It is difficult to give your cat all the water she needs this way, but often it can help get her started drinking. Some cats will let you give them fluids this way. Others may choose passive resistance, and let the water run out of their mouths. Or, they may stubbornly resist you. For these you have another option...

Give subcutaneous ("sub-q") fluids

If necessary, you can inject fluids subcutaneously - under her skin. Ask your your vet if sub-q fluids would help your cat. Your vet can also help you determine how much and how often to give your cat fluids, and show you how to do it. You will need needles, bags of Lactated Ringer's solution (or the equivalent), and (in my case) a second person to help: one to hold and pet the cat, the other to insert the needle and monitor the amount of fluid going in. It is also helpful to have something from which to hang the bag. I used an old camera tripod - adjustable and stable.

To give your cat fluids, get her sitting comfortably, pull up her skin near the nape of her neck, and insert the needle. Then open the drip valve and wait. Keep in mind the amount your vet recommended, but a little more or less should be fine (confirm with your vet!). You want to balance how much you give her with how many times you need to give it to her. When I have given fluids to my cat, I generally give about 100cc's, which takes just a few minutes. When she is done, praise her and give her a treat for sitting so patiently.

It can be a little nerve-wracking the first few times, but once you and your cat know what to expect, it can go quickly and easily. Our cat does not exactly look forward to it, but followed by treats, extra food and attention, it has become almost a spa treatment for her. Afterward, she eats better and seems more comfortable. She sleeps better, too, and that is well worth it.

One more hint: Warm the water before giving it to your cat by soaking the bag for a minute or two in a sinkful of warm water.

Collecting urine samples
To see the color of her urine, of course, you have to collect it. If you are "lucky" enough to have something she pees on outside the litter box, spread a thick plastic sheet underneath, and collect a sample from there. Otherwise, you can get hydrophobic sand for one-time collections, or a non-absorbent, washable litter, if you need to check her urine regularly.

Movement

As your cat ages, the running and jumping she once did so easily will grow more difficult. High places will be less accessible. She may strain to bend down for her bowls of food and water, too. Or she will fidget more before settling down for a nap, trying to get comfortable.

Basics

Play

As much as cats sleep, they still need to move, and not just to exercise, but to play, to hunt - to move for the joy of it. In other words, they need something to stimulate them physically *and* mentally.

She may not run as far or jump as high, but she will still enjoy swatting at a string, or pouncing on your hand moving under a blanket. It is also a way for you to spend time together, time that is not focused on her ailments. Play with her.

Comfort

When she is relaxing, take note of where she prefers to relax, and what she likes about it. Is it warmer - in a sunny window? Or cooler - under a chair on the deck? Is it a soft spot on a feather blanket? Is it smooth like a sheet? Or fluffy like fleece? Or nubby like a carpet? Is it a quiet spot away from the commotion of your household, or near the center of the action?

Does she prefer different spots at different seasons? At different times of day? Once you know, you can give her more of what she likes, and make it easier for her to get to her favorite spots (See *Use Ramps* under *Hints & Techniques*, below).

What to Watch

Does she still run and jump?

One of the first changes you will notice as your cat ages is that she won't frequent the high places she used to. When she was younger, that spot may have been the top of the refrigerator, a bookshelf, a window ledge. Or if she wanted to see what you were doing in the kitchen, she would just jump up and see for herself. But over time her favorite spot migrates to a sunny spot on the floor, and instead of jumping up she will paw at your leg to ask you to bend down.

Is her gait stiff?

Young cats walk smoothly and gracefully, but if your cat's joints hurt, she will not want to bend them as much. She may hop down stairs instead of striding. Or she may keep her back legs straight. Or *not* straighten her front legs. Any one of these is a sign that movement is not as easy and effortless as it used to be.

She may walk more slowly, especially up and down stairs. Or she may have difficulty keeping her pee inside the litter box.

Is she in pain?

Does she vocalize more? Or has her personality changed so she is more irritable? Does she keep more to herself than before? Any of these could be a sign that your cat is experiencing pain.

If this is the case, see your vet. Your vet may be able to uncover the underlying cause and offer treatments. There may also be dietary supplements that could help (like glucosamine and chondroitin). Ask your vet.

Hints & Techniques

Use ramps

Just because your cat can no longer jump up to high places does not mean she no longer likes high places. She just needs a way to get up and down more easily. Since you cannot always be there to pick her up and take her down when she wants, a ramp is the next best thing.

You can make your own, or buy one, just make sure it has a surface that is not too slippery, and that it is not too steep.

Add cushions

Sore joints and hard surfaces do not mix. Give your cat some extra padding so she can rest more comfortably. It does not need to be anything fancy - a pillow, a seat cushion, or a folded towel can all make a big difference. But do not make the padding so deep and soft that she sinks into the padding and has trouble getting back out. A firm cushion, or a soft cushion over a firm surface works best.

Use heating pads

A little extra warmth, especially during the cooler months, can ease your cat's stiffness. But be careful not to use heating pads designed for people - they can get too hot, and they are not designed to be laid upon. Heating pads for pets should not get hot, and will only warm when your cat is on them. Even then, if it is a warm summer day and she has found a sunny spot, your cat does not need the extra warmth of a heating pad, too. It may dry her out when she needs all the water she can get.

If she can get comfortable on or next to you, and you can stay still, *you* can make an ideal heating pad. If you have another cat who is willing to serve the same purpose, that works, too.

Massage

When you pet her, you can gently massage her. Find tender spots around her neck, shoulders and hips and rub with your fingertips. Keep the pressure light and make sure she is comfortable. You can also apply the same fingertip pressure along either side of her spine.

If she has trouble scratching an itch, you can scratch it, gently, for her. Always pay close attention to how she reacts. If she enjoys what you are doing, keep doing it. If she turns away or fidgets uncomfortably, stop.

Grooming

For your cat to groom herself requires a lot of flexibility. She needs to be able to reach all over her body with her tongue, and as she gets older it will be harder to reach certain areas.

Basics

Brushing and clipping
When she is young you should get in the habit of regular brushing and claw-clipping. How often you should do it depends on her coat - how long it is, and how prone to tangles and mats. It will keep her looking great, and it is also a great opportunity to check her coat and claws. You can spot parasites - fleas, ticks and mites; skin problems - rashes, dandruff, redness, growths; and problems with her feet and pads. Does anything look sore, red or swollen? Does she pull back or resist (more than usual) when you clip her claws?

Cleaning
Most cats do a good job of keeping themselves clean, but as they get older you will need to help. Pay special attention to your cat's face - eyes, ears, nose and mouth. You may need to clean them occasionally, gently, on the surface. I wet a few pieces of cotton, folded-up toilet paper or tissue, and wipe gently to remove any visible dirt. If she has problems with vomiting, check her front paws to remove any bile or residue there. And if she has problems with the litter box, you will also need to check and perhaps clean her bottom.

Check for problems
You should take note of anything that looks less than healthy and discuss it with your vet. It could be nothing, or it could be something serious. Your vet may suggest additional tests to know for sure. Even if it is something potentially serious, like a thyroid condition, it is often easy to manage or resolve if you catch it early.

What to Watch

Is her coat healthy?

Is her coat soft, lustrous and shiny? Or is it dry, dull, and matted? If her coat looks dull and lifeless it is a sure sign that she is not as healthy as she could be. It could simply be a matter of improving her diet, or it could be something more serious. You want her fur to be thick, lustrous and soft.

Is her skin healthy?

When you brush her, check underneath her fur. Is her skin soft and supple? Or does it seem dry? Does she have dandruff? Does she scratch or lick certain areas more than others? Is her skin red or irritated? Do you notice any unusual changes to her skin color, or any bumps or lumps?

Are her claws well-formed?

Is she still able to hone her claws on a scratching post? If she cannot her claws may thicken and fill in as new layers grow but the old layers are never rubbed off. When you press her paw pads to clip her claws does she pull her paws away (more than usual)? Is the sheath around the claw tender or swollen?

Are her teeth and gums healthy?

Check for strong, white teeth and healthy pink gums. If you feed her dry food, does she have trouble eating it? If you notice build-up on her teeth you should consider cleaning them, or ask your vet about options to get them cleaned.

Are her eyes, nose and ears healthy?

Do you notice anything unusual? Is there excessive wax in her ears? What color is it? Are her eyes watery? If your cat is prone to schmutzy ears or eyes, of course clean them, but note any changes in the amount, color or consistency of any discharge.

Hint/techniques

"Sponge" baths

Wet your hands and massage her. Start at her shoulders, reach your fingers around to her chest. Rub down her back. Scratch under her chin, wipe her face and rub her belly. If you do not have a faucet, or a sinkful of water nearby, use a misting bottle to keep your hands moist. You will gently clean her, remove loose fur and she will love it all at the same time.

It is also a perfect time to feel her body for anything unusual, to massage sore muscles and warm stiff joints.

Clip her claws

Older cats do not hone their claws as often as younger cats do, and you may notice that her claws are thick and rounded. Honing claws on a scratching post helps them shed their outer layer. When your cat can no longer hone them herself, her claws can grow thick and rounded, and may even push uncomfortably on her paws.

You can fix this easily when your clip her claws. After you clip her claw, hold it between two fingers and push gently on the inside of the arch of the claw. The loose layer should slide right off.

This also gives you a chance to check the condition of her feet and the sheaths surrounding her claws.

Because she does not run around as much as she used to, you may also need to trim her back claws occasionally. Use your judgment, but generally I clip only the tips off, when they start to click noticeably on hard floors.

Litter boxes

Litter boxes are not anyone's favorite thing to talk about, but they provide a very useful window into the inner workings of your cat. First, you have to make sure she keeps using it. Do this by making it easy to use. It should not be in a remote location, especially for an older cat. You may need to move it closer to her regular hangouts as she gets older so she can get to it quickly and easily.

Basics

The litter itself should be familiar to her. Changing cat litter - textures, materials, scents - can sometimes send your cat looking for new spots to use instead of the litter box.

You need to keep the box clean. You should have a good feel for how often and how much your cat leaves in her litter box. Clean up what she leaves behind often enough that she rarely has to use a box she has already soiled. And *thoroughly* clean the box regularly. Scrub and disinfect the plastic and replace the litter completely with fresh litter.

Sometimes, despite your - and your cat's - best efforts, she will have an accident and pee or poop outside the box. Of course clean those up immediately, but also try to figure out what might have caused the problem, and do what you can to prevent it from happening again. See *Hints & Techniques* below for a couple of ideas.

What to Watch

Can she use her box easily?
As she ages, a box that was easy to get to and get in may be more difficult to use. How can you tell? You can either watch her get in and out of the box, or look for accidents when you clean the box -

on the rim or just outside the box. In general, as she gets older she will prefer a box that is lower and larger.

Does she strain when she goes to the bathroom?
This could mean pain from arthritis, or she may need more water, or food that is easier to digest.

Does she use it regularly?
You know how much she eats, so you should have some idea what to expect in her litter box - how much and how often. If she starts going less often, it could be a sign of constipation or dehydration that should be investigated.

Is she consistent?
Are her poops about the same size, color and consistency? Are her pees about the same volume? You can help your vet assess your cat's condition if you keep an eye on this. Poops that are runny, or unusually dry, or black, or especially smelly, or anything different from what you have seen is worth at least a call to your vet. Excess urination could be a sign of a condition that needs treatment, such as kidney disease or diabetes.

Hints & techniques

Move litter boxes closer
The easier it is for her to get to the litter box, the more likely she will keep using it regularly, and not find a more convenient spot of her own.

Protect the floor around litter boxes
With stiffer joints, your cat may be unable to squat like she used to, and she may pee or poop over the sides of her box even though she does not mean to. You can use litter mats, but any water-resistant sheet will work, so long as it does not keep your cat away from the box. I have had good results with tar paper. You may also want to take measures to keep pee from running under the box, where it is harder to notice - and harder to clean up.

Get a larger litter box

To make access easier for your cat, you can also switch to larger containers for her litter box. I have used a cement mixing tub from the local home improvement store. It is inexpensive, and almost double the length and width of a regular litter box. Your cat, even with stiff joints, can still get in it comfortably and have plenty of room to pee without going over the side.

Get a shallower litter box

Sometimes getting in and out of a litter box is a challenge. In that case I use a washing machine drain pan. It is large - 32 inches square - but only 2 inches deep. To counteract her tendency to pee over the sides, keep the litter mounded in the center and away from the edges of the box.

Note: With larger boxes, make sure it is not too heavy or awkward for you to clean, empty and lift it.

Use diapers

If she can no longer make it to the box, diapers - washable or disposable - make it much more comfortable for her, and you won't need to wash her bedding due to accidents. Diapers are best if she is still moving around quite a bit, and you do not know where she might pee or poop.

Use absorbent bedding If she is not moving around much, it is more comfortable for her if you give her absorbent bedding and change it whenever she soils it. Layers work best to keep her dry and warm. On top of her heated, cushioned bed, add a waterproof plastic sheet, then an absorbent towel, and finally a non-absorbent fleece throw.

Medical care

Good veterinarians can be priceless - for their expertise, their guidance, and their expert care - but they are not the most important person in your cat's care. *You* are. You are the one who sees your cat every day. You are the one that can notice subtle changes in her behavior, her appearance, her movements. You can examine her any time, and you have plenty of time to do it thoroughly. And most important of all, she knows you, loves you and trusts you. You have been there for her for years, so she will let you examine her - and care for her - often in ways she would not tolerate from anyone else. And you can help keep her calm when others are treating her.

Basics

Your vet has been there to help you keep your cat healthy with vaccinations and regular examinations. Now, for your old cat, your vet can diagnose and treat her when she needs it.

But your vet can only do that if you do *your* job:

- *You* are the one who needs to know when to bring your cat to the vet.
- *You* provide follow-up care. Usually the vet prescribes a course of treatment. You have to follow through to make sure your cat gets what she needs. Whether it is a special diet, medicine (pills or shots), fluids, etc., you should make sure you understand what you need to do and know how to do it - before you leave the vet.
- *You* monitor your cat's healing. Whether it is progress, a slow decline, or a sudden turn for the worse, you need to be clear-eyed and clear-headed to let your vet know how your cat is doing.

- *You* advocate for your cat. If your cat is in pain, if your cat is struggling, if a treatment is not working, she is depending on you to get her the best care you can.

What to Watch

When you first get a diagnosis of some new condition in your cat it can feel overwhelming, or even hopeless, but there are many chronic conditions that can be managed. For example, asthma, kidney disease, hyperthyroidism, and diabetes all have treatments that can keep your cat happy and healthy for years after the diagnosis. Take a deep breath, learn as much as you can about your cat's condition, and you can handle it - together.

Hints & Techniques

Office, house-call and emergency vets
Maintain a good, ongoing, regular relationship with your cat's regular vet, but be aware of other options you might have. A mobile vet can help if your cat gets anxious leaving the house, and an emergency vet can be invaluable when issues crop up, as they often do, at night, on weekends, or over holidays.

Be calm, firm and gentle
Learn from your vet and your vet's assistants how to provide medical care to your cats. **Be calm.** The first time you have to treat your cat - to give her a shot, or take her blood to test her glucose - it can be nerve-wracking. But you will get better with experience. **Be firm.** Your cat may not want to get poked or prodded, so you will need to be firm in giving her care. She needs to know that she cannot easily brush you off. **Be gentle.** Understand that your cat does not feel as well as she could, and that treatment may be (initially) scary, or painful for her. Treat her as you would like to be treated. In fact, reward her with a treat when her treatment is done.

Pilling your cat, giving subcutaneous fluids, insulin shots
I was going to include descriptions of basic techniques here - how to pill a cat, give subcutaneous fluids, and so on, but these are better learned in person, from your vet.

Quiet Time

I know you are busy. I know your old cat needs you to do so many things for her - feeding and cleaning and medications and... But do not forget that both of you still need time just to be with one another, to feel close to each other - to pet her, if that is what she likes, or to sit nearby. Whatever her troubles, whatever your worries, they can wait. Now - right now - could last forever. Be there with her.

- Just pet her, or just sit with her. Do what she *wants*, not only what she needs.
- No feeding, no medicines, no brushing - unless she likes it.
- Love her and appreciate her.

Remember all the good times you have shared with her, but do not forget that she is still here, ready to make more memories with you.

Preparing for the inevitable

Sometimes... it is not enough

Sometimes you do all you can and still it is not enough, and your cat dies too soon. Remember, you did all you could, and you made her life healthier, happier and longer than it would have been without you. Take comfort in that.

When you are able, try to learn from the experience. Why did she die? Is there anything you could do for your other cats to keep the same thing from happening to them?

- If it was an accident, how can you make their environment safer?
- If it was an unknown health condition, is there any way to check if any of your other cats share the same condition?
- If it was a known health condition, are there any diet or medical remedies available now that were not before? Are there any preventative measures you could take to lower the risk of the same thing happening to your other cats?

Ultimately, we have to accept our limitations. There may be illnesses we fail to spot and treatments we do not give in time. But even if we could detect everything, even if we could know everything there is to know about our cat's health and condition, and do everything we could do for our cat, still there will come a time when there will be nothing we can do but let her go.

As that time approaches, provide comfort - warmth, safety, food and water, if she will take it - and love. Her life is a gift - a precious, one-of-a-kind, never-to-be-repeated gift, and she shared it with you. Thank her.

Making the call

First, do not be afraid to call the vet. With an old cat, it can be all too easy to fall into premature grieving when all your cat has is a cold, or an upset stomach. A little attention from a vet can (1) tell you if that is the case, and (2) put her quickly on the mend. If you are lucky enough to have a vet who will make house calls, it is a small price to pay for the health of your cat, and for your own peace of mind.

Second, do not be afraid of a natural death. If you can keep your cat comfortable, there is beauty - a sorrowful beauty - and dignity in a natural death. If you can, try to have the strength and courage to give it to her. Euthanasia - "putting her to sleep" - should not be for your comfort or convenience, but only as a last resort.

Whatever you decide, go with her as far as you can. She has been there for you, through all your ups and downs. Be there for her. She never needs to be alone.

After life

After you have said your final good-byes, you will grieve. She may leave a hole in your heart so big that you get three cats, and then a fourth, and still you miss them. You would think about them more often, if only it wouldn't make you cry.

There will be more time in the day - time without her - after she's gone. Time that you used to spend feeding her, cleaning her, caring for her and loving her will be... empty.

If you are lucky enough to have other pets, let them comfort you.

Be gentle with yourself, as she was gentle with you.

What if I die first?

You are taking such good care of your cat, that she may live long enough to outlive you. If that happens, how can you be sure that she gets the same care after you are gone?

You can provide for your cat in your estate plan. In the United States, depending on your state, you may be able to provide for her care in your will.

But most important, you will need people you trust - individuals, or no-kill shelters, who will give your cat a home. Talk to them now. Be sure they understand what you are asking of them, so they will be prepared. If you can, introduce your cat to them - so *she* will be prepared, too.

It may never be needed, but it is reassuring to know that your cat will be cared for, even if you can no longer do it.

Epilogue

Even if I had raised a hundred cats, or been veterinarian to thousands - and I have not, I would not know everything there is to know about caring for old cats.

In this short guide I have only scratched the surface - I hope in a useful, practical way. Has your experience been the same or different? Has my advice been helpful, or all wrong? Should I add something or take something out? I would love to hear from you!

Kurt Indermaur
<kurt+oldcatcare@viviculture.org>

Additional resources

Below are links to sites I have found useful over the years, either for information, for guidance, or for products for older cats. They are in no particular order, and I do not endorse them in any way other than that they helped me.

General cat care information

- Growing Old Gracefully[4] - "a guide for people owning or adopting older cats"
- Catster[5] - easy-to-read information on cat behavior, health and care
- Paws and Effect[6] - "a blog by cats, for cats and their people"

Cat health information

- Cornell University Feline Health Center[7] - articles and videos on a variety of feline health topics
- CatInfo[8] - information from a vet on feline health and nutrition
- PetMD: Dehydration in cats[9] - how to check for, treat and prevent dehydration in cats
- VirtuaVet provides stories from a practicing veterinarian to help you "remain confident, optimistic and happy in your healthcare decisions regarding your pet."

---

[4] http://www.messybeast.com/Oldcat.htm
[5] https://www.catster.com/
[6] https://paws-and-effect.com/
[7] https://www2.vet.cornell.edu/departments-centers-and-institutes/cornell-feline-health-center/health-information/feline-health-topics
[8] https://catinfo.org/
[9] https://www.petmd.com/cat/emergency/common-emergencies/e_ct_dehydration

    – VirtuaVet: How to tell if a cat is dehydrated[10]

    – VirtuaVet: Pet quality of life[11]

    – VirtuaVet: 19 year-old cat needs emergency dental surgery[12]
      - if you are hesitant about surgery for your older cat

Products to keep your cats comfortable and safe

- HandicappedPets[13] - for aging, disabled and injured pets
- SeniorPetProducts[14] - for older pets
- PetClassics[15] - furniture-quality ramps to help your cats get up to higher places
- PurrfectFence[16] - fencing to keep your cats safe outside

Veterinary supplies

- VetRxDirect[17] - veterinary supplies such as Lactated Ringers Solution, syringes, etc.
- 1-800-PetMeds[18] - more veterinary supplies, flea and tick treatments
- Doctors Foster and Smith[19] - veterinary supplies, as well as pet beds, heating pads and other products

---

[10]https://virtuavet.wordpress.com/2010/09/01/how-to-tell-cat-dehydration/
[11]https://virtuavet.wordpress.com/petqualityoflife/
[12]https://virtuavet.wordpress.com/2009/09/30/19yearoldcatneedsemergencydentalsurgery/
[13]https://www.handicappedpets.com/
[14]https://www.seniorpetproducts.com/
[15]http://www.petclassics.com/
[16]https://www.purrfectfence.com/
[17]https://www.vetrxdirect.com/
[18]https://www.1800petmeds.com/
[19]https://www.drsfostersmith.com/